I THINK YOU'RE ON MUTE

A STUDIO PRESS BOOK

First published in the UK in 2021 by Studio Press,
an imprint of Bonnier Books UK,
4th Floor, Victoria House, Bloomsbury Square, London WC1B 4DA
Owned by Bonnier Books,
Sveavägen 56, Stockholm, Sweden

www.bonnierbooks.co.uk

© Studio Press

1 3 5 7 9 10 8 6 4 2

ISBN 978 1 80078 247 1

Written by Ellie Ross
Edited by Saaleh Patel
Designed by Nia Williams
Production by Emma Kidd

A CIP catalogue for this book is available from the British Library
Printed and bound in Latvia

I THINK
YOU'RE ON
MUTE

A Foolproof* Guide to Living Your Best Online Life

*results may vary

 Ellie Ross

STUDIO
PRESS

CHAPTER 1
Work 5

CHAPTER 2
Personal 31

CHAPTER 3
Online Dating 58

CHAPTER 4
Social Media 85

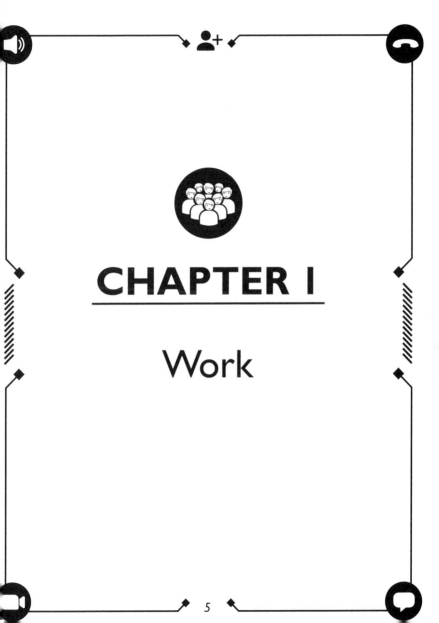

CHAPTER I

Work

How should I address an email?

Keep it simple. You can't go wrong with 'Hi [Name]' or 'Dear [Name]'.

Avoid:

Dear Sir/Madam – This has 'template email' written all over it

Hello – Are you reading from an English phrase book?

Hey – Save it for surf camp

Salutations! – Quirky isn't going to speed up my response

Greetings – There's an unspoken 'Earthlings' after this

When do I use 'To whom it may concern'?

When a company has ruined your life and you want to write them a *very* stern email about it.

How many people need to be in an email to warrant 'Hi All'?

One person? Easy. 'Hi [insert name]'. Two people? 'Hi Both'. Three? This is where it gets tricky. Three is not *all*. Three is some. But 'Hi Some' isn't an option. Four? We're getting closer, but I'd say you're in solid 'Hi All' territory with five recipients or more.

How should I sign off an email?

Again, don't overcomplicate it. 'Thanks' never goes out of style.

Avoid:

Take care – OK, Mr. Health & Safety!

Warm wishes – 'Warm'. Ew.

Best regards – It's Best wishes or Kind regards. Make your mind up.

Yours sincerely – This is just a little… intense.

Yours faithfully – What are you writing with, a quill?

I just ended an email to my boss with three kisses. What do I do?

Go with it. Three kisses? That's not embarrassing, it's chic! It's *European*!

What is appropriate attire for a Zoom meeting?

As the old adage goes: 'Dress for the job you want, not the job you have'. If that means showing up online in a spacesuit, so be it.

How do I choose a LinkedIn picture?

Easy. It just needs to be a photo of you looking warm and intelligent, taken by a professional photographer in natural lighting with a background that is plain yet engaging. You should be in 62% of the frame. Your eyes should be bright and hint at numerous hobbies, but no evidence of said hobbies should be in shot. Your smile should be friendly, with the ideal lip curvature being between 15-20 degrees. Showing teeth is fine if they are naturally white and straight. Try to adopt a facial expression that says you're a team player, you speak three other languages and are passionate about working overtime. Most importantly, relax. Don't overthink it.

What is a suitable Zoom background?

Your Zoom background should reflect your personality – provided your personality is interesting, intelligent, tasteful, well-travelled and stylish.

Include: a Farrow & Ball wall; a vintage foreign film poster; evidence of your generous donation to UNICEF.

Remove: framed photos from a recent nudist holiday; your china doll collection; your application for a new job.

How do I strike the right balance between informality and professionalism?

If you're thinking of adopting a more relaxed tone, start small and see how you go. It's easy to get too comfortable. One minute you're contemplating 'Cheers mate', and the next you're writing 'Spanks a mill' to the CEO.

Why has someone CC'd my boss into our emails?

Let's just say it's not because they want to organise post-work bevvies for the three of you.

How can I put this?

They think you're incompetent and want the world to know.

What do I do if I'm wearing pyjama bottoms on a video call but I need to stand up to go to the loo?

You can get away with anything if you do it with confidence. Lifting your bum a few inches off your chair and awkwardly side-shuffling out of view screams 'I'm wearing my Primark jammy bottoms with a baked bean stain down the front and I'd die if anyone saw'. Instead, rise slowly. Take your time. Saunter away with a cool poise that will leave your colleagues wondering where you bought your haute-couture athleisure from.

How can I increase my likeability in emails?

Try adding the word 'just'. See how it magically transforms 'Let me know' into 'Just let me know', or 'Wondering if you got my email' into 'Just wondering if you got my email'. With these four little letters, you'll be the office Nice Guy in no time!

At what point in an email exchange can I stop putting 'Dear Name'?

Nip it in the bud as soon as possible. Ideally after the first email. Otherwise you end up in a situation where you're firing emails to someone all morning – let's say they're called Robert and you're called Dave – every single one starts with *Hi Robert! / Hi Dave! / Hi Robert! / Hi Dave!* It's now a game of chicken and neither of you wants to be the first to drop it. When will this madness end?

Is it **OK** to mark an email as urgent?
URGENT

/ˈəːdʒ(ə)nt/

adjective

requiring immediate action or attention.

See also: dire; desperate; grave; critical; crucial

If you've read the definition above and still feel it applies to the content of your email (you need to let a client know you're on fire, for example) then you're totally within your rights to use it. If, however, you simply want a speedy response so you can clock off for Happy Hour at the Slug & Lettuce, I'm afraid it's a no.

Can I use acronyms at work?

If you're old enough to seek gainful employment then you're old enough to type the full phrase, TB perfectly H.

What phrases should I avoid in an email?

In a recent poll, the email phrase voted Most Annoying was…*drumroll*…

'I hope this finds you well.'

If you're struggling for an alternative however, don't panic. This is what a thesaurus is for. You might try:

I hope this finds you healthy.
I hope this detects you comfortable.
I hope this reveals you a hole in the ground from which to extract water.

The results aren't always perfect, but no-one can say you haven't tried.

Is there such a thing as too many exclamation marks?

Definitely! Use them wisely!! It's very easy to cross the line from breezy to unhinged!!!

How do I spell someone's name correctly?

As the Siobhans of the world will tell you, spelling a person's name correctly is not easy. Usually it's only in their email address as well as in their sign-off and possibly also their signature, so it's perfectly understandable to get it wrong…

Can I use my personal email address for work?

This depends on the email address. Don't expect promotion offers to come flooding in to lovemachine_99@hotmail.com.

What is a good synonym for 'unprecedented'?

Extraordinary; unparalleled; distinct; noteworthy; unique; strange; unrivalled, remarkable; weird; singular; uncommon; exceptional; abnormal; peculiar; unheard-of, idiosyncratic; anomalous; atypical. Bizarre. Bonkers. Bats. Bananas.

Anything — please God, anything — other than unprecedented.

How do I nudge someone for a response?

This lets them know it only occurred to you this very second that you hadn't received a reply yet. You have in no way been stewing on it for the past 48 hours.

Exclamation marks? Could you be any more breezy!

'Just checking you got my email! Let me know what you think whenever you get a sec! Thanks so much!'

You haven't even *finished* the word. That's how totes chillaxed you are.

Yup, you read that right. *Whenever*. Deadlines are for uptight losers. Which you definitely are not.

And there you have it. Your *third* exclamation mark in as many sentences. The person is left in no doubt that you are the most carefree, laidback, easy-going person on the planet. 'Does *nothing* bother you?' they'll be left wondering to themselves.

Should I keep the 'sent from my iPhone' signature?

There are two types of people who still use this. The first is your classic Baby Boomer. They've been given an iPhone by one of their children in an attempt to modernise their lifestyle ('now you can FaceTime the grandchildren!') but they haven't got a clue how to work the blessed thing. It takes them half an hour to write a text. Safe to say, this person can barely find the home screen let alone remove an email signature.

The other is Corporate Carl. Carl eats business deals for breakfast then flies to Milan for lunch. He is way too busy to be emailing from a desktop computer and *needs* you to know it.

I accidentally said 'Love you' at the end of a phone call to a colleague. What do I do?

This is up there with calling your teacher 'Mum', or replying 'You too' when your waiter tells you to enjoy your meal. In other words, embarrassing but not the end of the world.

And you never know, maybe after you hung up there was a pause, before they whispered 'You too' longingly down the line...

Myself and fifty others have been CC'd into an email – am I expected to reply?

Technically *readjusts spectacles* the CC function is for when the recipient needs to see information but a response is not required. And I would ask Martin from Accounts to kindly remember that.

What is the correct Mute etiquette on a video call?

We're still getting to grips with mute etiquette (metiquette?) but most of it is common sense. If you're a guest speaker and it's your turn to speak: unmute. If the meeting is just you and one other person: unmute. If there are 300 attendees, your baby's crying, or you're bitching about a colleague: mute. If you're eating: for GOD'S SAKE MUTE. The sound of you noshing that banana is like waves lapping against a shepherd's pie.

CHAPTER 2

Personal

I made a joke in a group chat and no one replied. Is there anything worse?

A few things. War, poverty, homelessness. Climate change. Anchovies. The film version of *Cats*.

Is there a cure for Zoom fatigue?

The annual number of minutes spent on Zoom is now over 3.3 trillion. That's a lot of minutes. No wonder we're tired.

Try these quick tips to fight the fatigue:

- Put your dog in a suit and have them stand in for you
- Practise blinking at least 200 times a minute to keep your heart rate up
- Wear a sleep mask and ear plugs in every call to trick your body into thinking you're getting some rest
- Do a shot every time someone says 'Sorry, I lost you for a second there!'
- Adopt different personas to keep things interesting. Russian spy? Soccer mom?
- Stay awake at night so that you're tired all the time, not just from Zoom

How can I get out of a virtual baby shower?

Sometimes honesty is the best policy. Tell your friend you love her and care deeply about her unborn child, but you'd rather lick a cowpat than play *Guess the Baby Weight!* over Zoom with her aunt.

What do I do if a friend calls me?

Fling your phone down the nearest well and run for the hills. Or just do what the rest of us do: stare at the screen until it stops ringing, then wait an appropriate amount of time before texting the person saying 'Hey! Sorry I missed your call, all OK? X'. Crisis averted (until next time).

What does my most-used emoji say about me?

The 'Crying with Laughter' Face

You love dogs, memes and true-crime documentaries. You can often be found saying 'No worries if not'.

The Poo

You're here for a good time, not a long time. You played the Artful Dodger in your school production of *Oliver!* and you once tried to capture a fart in a jar.

The Dancing Señorita

When you're not drinking prosecco at a bottomless brunch, you're posting a photo of a neon sign that says 'Well-behaved women rarely make history'. Starbucks is your favourite restaurant.

The Upside-down Smiley

Enigma's your middle name (or is it…?)

Where should my phone be when I'm in company?

Proper etiquette states that your phone should be switched off and placed inside a Ziploc bag, inside a safe, inside a locked room. Failing that, it should, at the very least, be in your pocket or bag. OK, it can be on the table, but the screen must be facing down. Or if it's facing up, you cannot look at it. If you *have* to look at it, no more than every ten minutes. Definitely no more than every five minutes. Every three minutes, tops. That way everyone knows they have your undivided attention.

Should I set up a WhatsApp group?

WhatsApp groups are great in principle. Distant relatives united! Book club chats galore! Except the world has gone WhatsApp-thread mad. Group chats have multiplied like bacteria on a three-day-old piece of ham. Now, people set up a WhatsApp group to let you know they're going to set up a WhatsApp group. I'm not saying you shouldn't, but be mindful. Know that the participants are probably wading through 40 other threads at the same time. Which brings us on to the next question…

Is it rude to leave a WhatsApp group?

It's not, but WhatsApp likes to play mind games by pretending it is. 'Steve has left the group' leaves us wondering what's wrong with Steve. He's so dramatic. He didn't even say goodbye.

Chances are Steve just doesn't want to receive Stag Do spam about a Stag Do he can't make. Fair enough, Steve. Fair enough.

Can I have my phone on loud?

Home? Yes.

Library? No.

Phone shop? Yes.

Yoga class? No.

Supermarket? Yes.

Funeral? No.

I'm waiting for a response and can see the other person has been Typing for five minutes. Can I ask them to hurry up?

But then they'll see you're typing and stop typing to let you finish typing. And you're only typing to ask them to keep typing, which you wouldn't need to type if they'd stopped typing. So you stop typing and wait for them to start typing again, but they've done the same. Now no-one's typing.

Why is a website telling me my password is too weak?

Take no notice. Bullies like this website thrive on making others feel bad. Your password might be strengthily-challenged but our imperfections are what make us unique.

I can see that someone has read my message, but they haven't replied. Do they hate me?

I'm afraid the most likely answer is yes. It's the only explanation. (There is of course a minuscule chance that they are busy, but hatred is way more logical.)

Do I sound as bad on my voicemail greeting as I think I do?

Probably. I'm sorry.

Is it ever **OK** to use Google in a pub quiz?

This is usually considered a big no-no, but I can understand the temptation. There's nothing more demoralising than staring blankly at the answer sheet like a GCSE exam you haven't revised for, while slipping down the leaderboard until even the group of students in the corner called 'Grin and Beer It' are beating you. In this case, it's not cheating, it's survival.

Do I really need to register with a GP when Dr Google's in my pocket?

Tempting as it is to believe the internet when it tells you your splinter is possibly, probably, definitely, a symptom of a rare and fatal tropical disease, it's still worth asking a professional. It's unlikely that @doccy4u has a PhD.

Am I a Phubber?

Coined in 2012, phubbing is a portmanteau for phone snubbing, aka ignoring someone because you are on your phone. Watch out for this. It's far better to be Grompany (great company) or an Attistener (attentive listener).

Is it acceptable to make a phone call on the train?

One of life's great mysteries is why it's fine for two friends chat to each other, but not for one person to chat on the phone. My theory? We're nosy bloody bastards. We don't mind people in our carriage having a good old chinwag because we can hear the whole thing. But spending the entire journey from Reading to Exeter listening to: 'You're kidding?!...Oh she never!...Then what?...You're kidding?!' It drives us mad. Put it on speakerphone or put a sock in it.

Should I answer a withheld number?

Sure! Go for it! Take a risk! Live fast and loose, baby!

I'm at a dinner party and everyone is talking about algorithms. Should I admit I don't know what they are?

No need. Say: 'Ah, I see we're talking about computer programs that extract data from our internet behaviours to determine what content we're shown', then steer the conversation onto how moist the chicken is.

Is it **OK** to have my camera turned off in a video call with mates?

Would you put a paper bag over your head at a party?

I love my parents but how can I tell them I don't love talking to their ear/double chin/the wall?

If your parents haven't quite mastered the art of the video call, be patient with them. You'll understand in twenty years, when your own kids are frustrated with you for not knowing how to adjust the Virtual Reality settings of your bionic eye.

Should I check my partner's phone?

We all know the best relationships are built on trust. And what better way to build trust than collecting cold, hard evidence. Leave no stone (or messaging app) unturned. My motto for feeling secure and happy is: Believe Nothing, Question Everything. Is 'I'm hot and I'm on my way' really from Dominoes? It's your duty to find out. Godspeed, Sherlock.

How can I limit my screen time?

Water your plants. Bake a cake. Buy a Rubik's Cube. Count the hairs on your head. Count the hairs on your arm. Write your Dragon's Den pitch. Master the phonetic alphabet. Learn how to pronounce Matthew McConaughey. Work backwards in sevens from one million. Hold your breath. Read War and Peace. Twice. Pole dance. Morris dance. Tap dance. Have twins.

Is it rude to be on the phone when you're being served at the till?

As long as you balance your phone awkwardly in the crook of your shoulder, mouth 'sorry' at least five times and perfect the 'will this person ever stop talking?' eyeroll, you should be fine. The trick is to let the cashier know that you know you're an arsehole.

Do I have Nomophobia?

Nomophobia is the fear of being without your phone. If you're anxious about whether you're anxious, you probably have it.

CHAPTER 3

Online Dating

How do I get a good Tinder photo?

DO

Pose with less attractive friends

Beg, borrow or steal a puppy

Photoshop in the Taj Mahal

Grab a Sharpie for some cute DIY freckles/hipster ink.

DON'T

Choose a photo taken on a Blackberry

Overdo the peace sign

Draw attention to your ankle tag

Pose with your husband or wife

If in doubt, be really, really attractive.

What should I include in my bio?

If your own life's a little dull, don't be afraid to 'borrow' from Wikipedia. Babes will come flocking to hear how you invented the telephone in 1876.

Is it acceptable to stretch the truth in my profile?

It's OK to put 'Non-smoker' even though you enjoy the odd menthol after a few drinks, or to turn one holiday to Magaluf into 'Loves to travel'. But stick within the realms of reality. I once went on a date with a guy who said he wrote the lyrics to Bohemian Rhapsody. He wasn't born at the time (and more importantly, wasn't Freddie Mercury).

How can I tell who the profile belongs to when all their photos are group shots?

It's easy to be put off by this (we get it, you've got mates) but look at it another way: it's a dating Lucky Dip! Ooh! Which mystery man or woman could be yours? The redhead in blue? Shorty pulling the peace sign? Dude on the left wearing fake Ray Bans?

I'm a single male. Should I state my height?

Absolutely*.

*as long as you're over 6'2.

I swiped right by accident – now what?

This is a lose-lose situation. Either they also swipe right and you're stuck with an unappealing match that you wouldn't date if they were the last person on Earth. Or they swipe left, leaving you off the hook. Phew, right?

Wrong. That means they swiped left. On you. Ouch.

I swiped left by accident – now what?

It's a Sunday night and you are idly browsing Tinder on the sofa. Your thumb is on autopilot, rhythmically swiping left. No. No. No – wait, YES! I meant Yes! Come back!

But it's too late. They've gone. In that split second, your future life together flashes before your eyes: strolling along a beach at sunset; affectionally dabbing jam on the end of each other's noses as you eat breakfast in bed; the adorable Cavapoo you would have called Teddy. All turned to dust.

Will you ever forget them? No. But will you find happiness anyway? Probably not.

Who should make the first move?

The Victorian Age called: they want their question back.

What's a good conversation starter?

As the old saying goes: never talk about religion, politics or money. As the new saying goes: never talk about religion, politics, money, Brexit, Trump, medical issues, office gossip, sex, death or your ex. Best stick to 'Hi'?

How do I make The Transition?

There might come a time when you want to move from messaging on the app to WhatsApp or text. This the online equivalent of saying 'What say you and I take this somewhere a little quieter?!' If you don't feel brave enough to ask outright, one option is to fake a technical glitch. 'Sorry, my app's playing up, any chance you could hit me up on this number?' Smoooooth.

If I'm messaging someone, how long should I leave between replies?

Life's short. Reply whenever you're free. If you want to play games, buy a Nintendo.

I thought I'd really clicked with someone, so why have they stopped messaging/ignored my suggestion to meet up?

May I refer you gently and tactfully to the 2009 movie *He's Just Not That Into You*.

I've seen someone I know on a dating app, what do I do?

Someone you know as in the cute barista who works at your local coffee shop, or someone you know as in your best friend's fiancé? Context is everything here.

How can I tell over chat whether it's worth meeting someone in person?

Open with a joke. This immediately sorts the wheat from the chaff. There are three responses to look out for. Scenario A – the Holy Grail – is that they respond with a joke. They get your humour and even better, they're funny too. Could they be The One? *cue humming the wedding march* Scenario B: they reply with 'Haha'. This isn't the world's best banter but we can work with this. This isn't terrible. Definitely worth exploring further. Scenario C: they do not get the joke. The ultimate red flag.

Let's look at an example: You see your match's profile picture is them with their Gran.

You say: 'Which one's you in that photo?'

Response A: 'I'm the short one with grey hair. Lockdown hasn't been kind to me.' OK, it's hardly *Live at the Apollo*, but they're up for the hashtag banter. Winner winner chicken dinner.

Response B: 'Haha'. Self-explanatory.

Response C: 'I'm on the left?? The other person is my Gran!' Unmatch and delete. You haven't got time for this.

I think my match is chatting to other people. Is it OK to ask?

If you think someone is Benching you (keeping you as a substitute while they trial other players, so to speak) there's no harm in finding out. But stay calm. You're not in a committed relationship and they're not technically doing anything wrong.

Avoid saying:
Who the hell is she?
Do I mean nothing to you?
I was ready to give you everything!
What am I going to tell my mother?
The wedding is officially OFF.

When's a good time to send someone a dick pic?

Quarter past absolutely never. We don't need it, we don't want it, we don't deserve it.

It's worth noting that even if you feel *absolutely certain* someone would like to receive one, hold fire. First impressions matter. Trust me when I say that whatever you've got tucked down your Y-fronts will look a lot more appealing after dinner and cocktails than in some blurry snap taken in a poorly-lit bathroom.

I'm a nurse and my partner's a fireman. How do I tell my grandparents we met on Sexyuniforms.com?

Ignorance is bliss. Tell Granny and Gramps your eyes met over the buffet at a barn dance, and the rest is history.

How do I know if I'm being catfished?

Unfortunately, the nature of a catfish means you won't know until you meet them. But there are red flags to look out for: the Getty Images logo, for instance.

How do I know if I'm a catfish?

Tell-tale signs your own photo may not be a true likeness:

It was your profile picture when MySpace launched

Your mum wouldn't recognise you

You now have half the amount of hair follicles

It's a photo of someone else

One way to be absolutely certain you're not misleading anyone is to use a passport photo. It's not sexy, but damn it, it's honest.

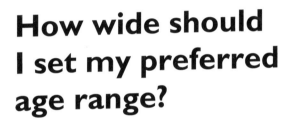

How wide should I set my preferred age range?

18-99. Why put a limit on love?

Someone has asked me to send nudes. Should I?

Sure, why not? A fine Botticelli might be appreciated, or perhaps Michelangelo? Or a Lucian Freud, if his tastes are a little more modern. Or Matisse! He does some fun paintings of—Sorry? What do you mean he means *of yourself*?

Should I check my match's social media page before our date?

This is a no-brainer. Not looking up someone online before meeting in person is like not viewing a house before you put in an offer to buy. What if you have a brilliant date, then you find out they troll C-list celebs on Twitter or their cover photo says 'Live, Laugh, Love'?

Is it ever OK to Ghost someone?

Casper has a lot to answer for: Ghosts are never friendly. Do the right thing. There's a human being behind that screen and their feelings are at stake. This person deserves to know the truth: that you are moving to Tasmania on a secret work mission tomorrow morning and your mobile phone and all other means of contact will be confiscated indefinitely.

Why am I being Haunted?

The supernatural can't always be explained. Let me tell you a story. Once upon a time, Linda was dating the wonderful Darren, when... poof! Without warning, he stopped messaging. No texts, no WhatsApps, nothing. Linda wondered anxiously what terrible fate might have befallen him, before realising he had blocked her number. That's when she knew: Darren was a Ghost. But one stormy night, alone in her flat, Linda heard a noise coming from her phone... The window panes rattled as she picked up the device. Her heart froze. It... it was Darren. Back from the dead. He had liked her latest Instagram post, despite months of no contact. She never found out why, but legend has it that he still Haunts her social media pages to this day.

I've been on several dates with a match. Should I delete my dating apps?

Whoa there, tiger. Let's not make any rash decisions. Don't put all your eggs in one basket (or take all of your eggs out of the basket?) until you know you're both on the same page. What if you're planning matching tattoos while they still check Tinder when you've gone to the toilet?

CHAPTER 4

Social Media

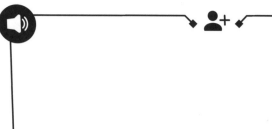

Am I too old for Tick Tock?

It's spelled TikTok. I think you have your answer right there.

Is it safe to say what I really think on Twitter?

Expressing your opinion in a Tweet is like lighting a firework. You should be fine if you follow safety procedures, but it's important to be aware of the dangers. Follow these guidelines to avoid unnecessary explosions:

1) Pace yourself by lighting one fuse at a time

2) Never point it directly at another person

3) Once lit, immediately retreat six feet

4) Don't be distracted by excitable spectators

5) Keep children away from the site

6) Sober is safer

7) If you're messing around, someone is likely to get hurt

8) If in doubt, leave it to the professionals

I liked a post by mistake. Can I unlike it?

Unlike-ing something is quite a statement. It says 'My thumb accidentally suggested I find you humorous/interesting/attractive, but I want to make it perfectly clear that I don't.' Anyway, you don't have a finite stash of double clicks. Go nuts! Scatter those likes around like sprinkles on a cupcake and go to sleep knowing you've put a bit more love into the world.

Should I delete a drunk Tweet?

Yes. And then you need to sit White Wine down and demand answers. Why on earth did she think it was a good idea to encourage you to post: 'what do m y boss and rhe vaccine have In common ? they 're both small prickss'.

How do I get more Instagram followers?

The important thing is quality not quantity of followers. Look at Jesus Christ – he only had twelve.

How can I create a viral video?

The idea of anything spreading through society like – well, like a virus, is not quite as alluring as it once was. The world has had quite enough of that, thanks.

When's a good time to post the results of a personality quiz?

Repeat after me: No-one, and I mean no-one, is interested in what biscuit you'd be if you were a biscuit.

Am I addicted to Snapchat filters?

Is the sight of your face in its natural state enough to make you break into a cold sweat? Do you crave that sweet, sweet high of adding bear ears/a floral crown/exploding heart eyes? If so, you might have a problem, but admitting you need help is the first step. With acceptance comes recovery. There'll come a time when you can and you will post a photo without a dog's nose.

How can I avoid mindless scrolling?

Set strict time limits. That way, when you end up on your ex's new girlfriend's sister's social media page, looking through her holiday photos from 2014, you've only got seven minutes (and counting) to do so.

I've been seeing someone for a while. Is it still cool to update my relationship status on Facebook?

Was it ever?

Could I be an influencer?

Take our quiz to find out! Score one point for each statement that describes you.

1) I'd rather eat cold food than not take a photo of it first.

2) Latte art is the new actual art.

3) It's not an event without a balloon arch.

4) A lot of people have asked about my skincare routine.

5) It makes sense to remortgage my house to buy a drone.

6) I genuinely feel #blessed.

0-1

I'm afraid you couldn't influence a nun to wear black.

1-3

You can give it a shot. Try something simple, like starting an Instagram story with 'Hey lovelies, sorry I've been quiet on here recently…'

4+

Honey, what are you waiting for? Go get that #sponsorship!

How can I protect myself against targeted ads?

Avoid talking to anyone about your hobbies or tastes or interests or likes, or any commodity you use, or have used, or thought about using once. In fact, avoid talking altogether. Thinking is safe in moderation, but try to limit thoughts to only those which allow you to perform essential daily tasks. Anything else can (and will) pop up on your Instagram feed.

Am I posting too many Facebook updates?

Only you know how much you're comfortable sharing, but if Jen from the year below at school knows what time you had a KitKat this morning, it might be time to cut back (on updates, not KitKats).

How can I cull Facebook friends without causing offence?

It's unlikely that anyone you want to unfriend (old school friends, ex-colleagues, someone you met in a hostel eleven years ago) will notice or care. Face it, you've probably been on their cull list for years.

Should I let a celebrity know I don't like them or what they do?

A troll is small, green, warty guy who lives under a bridge and terrorises humankind.

Don't be that guy.

Yesterday I forgot to Skip Ad on YouTube. How can I get those 30 seconds back?

I'm afraid you can't, and you shouldn't torture yourself trying. We all make mistakes. You're not the first person to watch an entire yoghurt advert and sadly, you won't be the last.

Should I ask Hun if they're OK?

Hun's status has prompted concern and like the caring person you are, you want to enquire into their wellbeing. You are a good citizen and an empathetic cyber-friend. But let's think this through. First and foremost, how well do you know Hun? If the answer is not very, take a moment to consider your motives. Secondly, assuming Hun is not OK, what next? Are you truly willing to be Hun's support? Don't offer a slice if you're not prepared to bake the pie. Finally, bear in mind that Hun might not actually want to share their problems. Sometimes Hun simply needs to post a cryptic message and get it out of their system.

My phone's run out of battery – how will I take photos?

You can either keep an emergency watercolour set to hand, or – and hear me out for a second – don't take any photos. I once heard that if you're on a hen do/ at a Coldplay concert and you don't take photos, you are in fact still on the hen do/ at the Coldplay concert. This might just be a rumour but there's only one way to find out...

What should I write in a caption?

Can't think of anything interesting to say? Use our handy Cliché Caption Generator to help you out! Just close your eyes and see where your finger lands.

Sunday funday	Rosé all day	With this one
No caption needed	Goals	So this happened
About last night	Not a bad view	Shameless selfie

I've made a new friend in real life. When can I follow them on social media?

Forget romance – new friendships are the best. You're positively giddy to have found each other! How empty your days must have been before you met! That's why it can be nerve-wracking to take the next step and befriend them online. Firstly, you don't want to seem too keen. Is it too keen? Maybe you should wait. Or should you just do it? Fuck it, you've done it. And now the real fear sets in. Will they still like you when they know how many photos you post of your cat?

How do I know if people want to see a photo of my coffee?

Unless they say 'I want to see a photo of your coffee', assume they don't.

See also:

How do I know if people want to see a photo of my sourdough?

How do I know if people want to see a photo of my plane window?

How do I know if people want to see a photo of my Aperol Spritz?

What's a good quote to post?

Anything by Marylin Monroe/Steve Jobs/Gandhi should do the trick. It's not about the words anyway. What matters is that you are inspiring. You are motivating. Your followers are lost souls and they need to hear the words of others through the medium of you.

What is the purpose of a hashtag?

In the olden days, the hashtag was a way of connecting like-minded people or allowing us to explore hobbies online. It was all so wholesome. #wildlife, #baking, #photography, #crochet. This is what the creators had in mind. But it has since taken on a life of its own and the results aren't always pretty.

Top offenders:

#bestdayever – #boastymcboasterson

#takemeback – Who are you asking? You haven't even said please.

#nofilterneeded – It might not have needed one, but did you use one? Because that golden glow looks suspiciously like Valencia.

#firstworldproblems – I don't live in a developing country! LOL!

#newhairdontcare – If you don't even care, how can you expect the rest of us to?

Is there a limit on how many photos I should post of myself working out?

If you're concerned, speak to your GP. It sounds like you could have a case of Gymselfieitis. This is an increasingly common condition and generally affects people between the ages of 21 and 35. Other symptoms include the loss of your T-shirt, involuntary flexing of muscles and the compulsion to include hashtags such as #noexcuses, #backatit and #legday.

Should I ask permission before I post a photo of someone?

Definitely. We've all been the wrong side of this: you wake up from a Big Night Out with a pounding head. There's garlic sauce on your pillow. You pick up your phone to see how quickly Deliveroo can dispatch a McMuffin when you spot the notification: you've been tagged in a photo. You open the app. It's worse than you feared. You look shinier than a roll of tin foil and one eye is half-closed. A button's come off your shirt. Your hair is a shit-show. Needless to say, everyone else in the photo looks like a Victoria Secrets' model. There should be a law against this.